The Art of Throwing Weapons

The ART OF THROWING Weapons

James W. Madden
Paladin Press • Boulder, Colorado

The Art of Throwing Weapons
by James W. Madden

Copyright © 1991 by James W. Madden

ISBN 0-87364-841-2

Printed in the United States of America

Published by Paladin Press, a division of
Paladin Enterprises, Inc., P.O. Box 1307,
Boulder, Colorado 80306, USA.
(303) 443-7250

Direct inquiries and/or orders to the above address.

FOR MARCI

CONTENTS

PREFACE

Thinking back many years, I can still remember when my father gave me my first real knife. I was a Cub Scout at the time and the knife was a Cub Scout pocket knife. That knife went everywhere that I went. Although it was not much of a throwing knife, it spent many hours bouncing off trees. The thrill I would feel when the knife finally stuck into a tree is a sensation I still have trouble explaining.

Perhaps part of that sensation came from the fact that for the first time in my life I felt some type of physical control over things outside my immediate reach. I felt the same kind of excitement by breaking a bottle with a rock from thirty feet or by hitting a target with an arrow from across the yard. I have found that this same sensation is shared with and sought after by a great many other people, and I feel that it goes back to a very primitive time in man's past.

In the years since obtaining my Cub Scout knife, I have met many people who have shared my interest in throwing knives, as well as tomahawks, spears, and other primitive weapons. Oddly enough, although interest in these weapons appeared to be widespread, the knowledge of how to throw them correctly was not. Written material on throwing weapons seemed almost non-existent or at best very sketchy, and experts were few and far between. It seemed as if throwing weapons was almost a lost art.

As my interest continued to grow, I spent many hours practicing, experimenting, and talking to people who were knowledgeable and informed about the art of throwing weapons. Additionally, I read whatever material was available on this subject. With time and practice, I was able to work out the basic fundamentals for throwing many different types of weapons. I have spent many enjoyable hours pursuing this hobby and sharing it with others, and I would like to share it with you now.

Along with learning the technical aspects of throwing weapons, I found the history and development of these early weapons quite fascinating.

Rather than simply present a manual on how to throw these weapons, I have also included some of the historical and developmental background of these weapons. By doing this, I hope to provide you with an interesting and well-rounded approach to the art of throwing weapons.

James W. Madden

1.
THROWING WEAPONS

Sit back and try to imagine this scene. It is a misty morning two million years ago on the Serengeti Plain of East Africa. A small band of primitive men foraging for food are suddenly surprised by a hungry lion. With nowhere to run, members of the group huddle together in fear behind their leader. He carries a large stick, pointed at one end, and in desperation he hurls it at the advancing animal. The staff strikes the lion a glancing blow, but nevertheless it causes him to flee. The group's leader is now a hero, and soon other members of the primitive band are carrying large pointed sticks.

No one will ever know for sure just how or when men first came to use weapons, but there can be little doubt as to what these weapons were. The first weapons of man were crudely formed from rocks, branches, bones, and antlers into spears, clubs, axes, and other basic weapons. When held in the hand these weapons extended a man's reach, increased his leverage, and provided either a sharp, a pointed, or a hard surface with which to strike another man or beast. These simple hand-held weapons were a major advancement for mankind enabling him to become more competitive in his fight for survival. It was not however until man learned to throw these weapons that his niche as a predator in the environment was greatly expanded. First of all, men found that they could hunt and kill animals which had been too swift or too large to be of any use to them. Secondly, they found it possible to make a kill from a safer distance with less risk to themselves. In time, with these simple Stone Age weapons, and with his increasing intelligence, man was transformed from a quiet, timid creature into the most ferocious predator on Earth.

Throughout the centuries numerous throwing weapons have been developed in many different cultures and lands. Many times the same or similar weapons were developed simultaneously or independently in different places thousands of miles apart. It is interesting to note that the types of throwing weapons found in certain areas seemed to have evolved in order to suit the needs of a particular people in a particular location and environment. Boomerangs and throw-sticks for example would be almost useless in a jungle environment. However on the deserts and plains of Australia, Egypt, or the southwestern United States, they have been used for thousands of years as they are an ideal weapon for these surroundings. On the other hand weapons such as the spear and the axe are so practical and useful that they have appeared in one form or another in every culture up to and including our modern age.

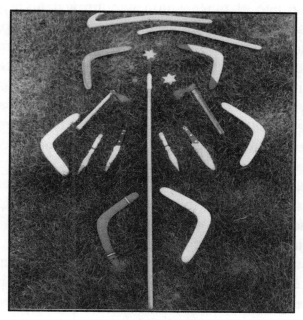

Figure 1.1
Assortment of throwing weapons

It might seem strange then that these basic throwing weapons which evolved along with man and were of such critical importance to man for thousands of years seem so awkward in the hands of most modern men. Spears, axes, throwing stars, and boomerangs are obsolete as weapons in a modern society. Today we buy our meat in grocery stores and if men go to war they go in tanks and airplanes. They carry rifles and grenades rather than spears and tomahawks. It would be wrong however to think that the art of making, handling, and throwing these simpler weapons is a totally lost art. The reverse is true. New interest in learning to make and throw these simple, basic weapons is growing day by day.

In the age of push button warfare and high-powered rifles, men apparently are finding it a challenge to develop these older skills once again. Mountainmen organizations and other outdoor clubs throughout the country often hold competitions in throwing tomahawks, knives, and spears along with their other activities. Some sportsmen are even learning to hunt again with spears, knives, and boomerangs. With the growing interest in the martial arts, many people are finding throwing shurikens (throwing stars) or knives to be an interesting and challenging activity. All of these activities appear to be growing in popularity, but the principles and fundamentals of throwing these weapons are lost to most people and must be taught anew.

There are basic fundamentals in throwing weapons as there are in other sports. You must first learn these basics to gain maximum effectiveness and to keep from developing bad habits. This book will teach you these fundamentals. Each chapter will elaborate on the proper way to grip or hold each weapon, the proper stances, and the throwing motions from start to finish. These are the basics and if executed correctly these basics will produce good throws time after time for everyone.

In an effort to give an overall view, some of the history and developments as well as the throwing techniques used will be examined for each type of throwing weapon. I have chosen five types of weapons which in recent years seem to have become the most popular. Each weapon is covered in a separate chapter. The weapons are the spear (sometimes referred to as the lance or javelin); throwing knives; the tomahawk (throwing axe); shurikens (throwing stars); and the boomerangs.

Figure 1.2
*Hanging target used for spears, knives, tomahawks and
shurikens*

Each chapter will also emphasize the importance of **safety** in regard to these weapons. These are all dangerous weapons and precautions must be observed. First of all, enough space must be allowed so that there is no danger of hitting another person or pet. Causing damage to property by wild throws or ricochets must also be avoided. Proper targets made of boards or circles cut from trees are also important to have when throwing spears, knives, tomahawks, and shurikens. If these weapons are taught at Scout camps or other outdoor schools proper supervision and instruction should be provided just as it would be at the archery or rifle range. The making, care, and maintenance of weapons and targets ought to be included in such a course. It is important to remember that these are all weapons and that good judgment, common sense, and care must be practiced.

For the sake of simplicity I have assumed throughout this book that the reader will be throwing these weapons with his right hand. If you are left-handed, merely substitute the word left for right and right for left whenever instructions are given. The approach used here will be practical and not highly technical. I will not elaborate on the aerodynamics of the weapons in flight, but I will tell you about the weapons and how to throw them. Given the proper equipment and the basic fundamentals as presented here, anyone willing to put in the necessary hours of practice can become proficient with any or all of these weapons. I think you will find your time spent involved in these activities to be interesting and entertaining.

2.
THE SPEAR OR LANCE

Imagine one day you were to find yourself a victim of a shipwreck or an aircraft mishap and you are stranded in an African savanna, a jungle in Brazil, or perhaps in the Alaskan wilderness. You are left with only the clothes on your back, the abundance of nature, and your own ingenuity and resourcefulness. What would be the one weapon that you could make that would be the most useful and effective both for hunting and for protecting yourself from predators? If your choice was the spear or lance, you made the correct choice. Your chances for surviving your ordeal would be greatly improved.

With the exception of rocks, the spear or lance was by far the most primitive and widespread of all hunting and throwing weapons. The spear is such an ideal weapon that if it was not passed on from prior generations, it would certainly have been independently developed many times over throughout the world. The spear offered many advantages and was for thousands of years a perfect weapon for early man. First of all the spear was easy to make and was very effective either held or thrown. The spear also enabled man to kill larger and swifter animals and to kill from a safer distance. Man thus became a much more efficient hunter and this greatly improved his chances for survival.

In time as civilizations advanced and effective longbows, crossbows, and later guns were developed, the spear became obsolete in many cultures. It was quickly discarded in favor of current weapons. Skills developed over hundreds of thousands of years were soon all but forgotten by most men. In the most primitive cultures throughout the world however, the spear in one form or another has survived and is still used today. With the encroachment of civilized man on almost all corners of the earth, more and more of these native people are laying down their spears. These primitive hunting and gathering societies are feeling the pressures of civilization. Many are being converted to a more modern way of life.

Although the use of the spear worldwide is rapidly declining as a necessary primitive weapon, its popularity is increasing as a sport and as a means of recreation. The javelin for example is a type of spear designed to be thrown a long distance with accuracy not being a major factor. The javelin throw is a popular event in track and field, and it is one of the ten events in the modern decathlon. The spear which we are concerned with in this chapter however is the traditional hunting spear which was used by primitive men to insure their day to day survival.

Different variations of hunting spears have been developed and used to suit the individual needs of many different cultures. The most versatile and common type of lance or hunting spear is the light spear. This spear was universally used by early men including the North American Indians.

The light spear was not heavy enough to be a burden to carry on hunting trips but it could bring down anything from a rabbit to a deer, and if necessary, it could effectively be used against large predators or other men.

The light spear is usually 4 to 7 feet long and 3/4 to 1 and 1/2 inches in diameter. The points of the earliest spears were simply sharpened and then hardened by fire. Sharp bones or antlers were sometimes fastened to the end of the spear. The most reliable spearheads of this early age were fashioned from flint, chert, obsidian and other sharp rocks. These stone spearheads were often made with a high degree of skill and proved to be extremely sharp and deadly. For many thousands of years, they were the best points available until metals were discovered and introduced into ancient societies and cultures.

MAKING A LIGHT SPEAR

The light spear which I make and throw is much like the ones I have been describing. For practical reasons I make these spears with steel points. Although antler and stone points are very useful when the goal is to pierce animal flesh, they do not hold up well when thrown at wooden targets. The best steel points are sturdy, inexpensive throwing knives (8 to 10 inches long) available in sporting goods stores and knife shops. For the shaft of the spear I use heavy duty broom handles which are available in any hardware store. These poles are made of pine and are usually about 5 feet long and less than an inch in diameter. A straight pole like this will make a perfect shaft for your spear.

At one end of the shaft I cut a slit through the center approximately 4 and 1/2 inches deep and 1/8 of an inch wide to fit the knife handle.

This leaves the point protruding about 5 and 1/2 inches. The size of this cut will vary according to the type of point you choose to use.

I put the shaft into a large vise and then use a saber saw or a hand saw to cut the slit. Next the handle of the knife is inserted into the slit and the area is packed with wood putty. It should be allowed to dry perfectly straight. When the wood putty is dry and the rough spots sanded, coiling a light cord tightly around the split end of the shaft will provide added reinforcement to the blade. Shellacking the cord or giving it a light gluing and allowing it to set for a day is the last step in making a light spear. This method of spear making will make a very durable spear which will withstand a great deal of stress and punishment. You may or may not need to adjust the length of your spear. The optimum or ideal length for your spear will depend on many factors such as your own size and strength. Trial and error will work best to determine the proper length. For this reason it is best to leave the shaft a little long and to shorten it until it feels right. Your spear is now ready to throw: find and open space, a suitable target, and let's go!

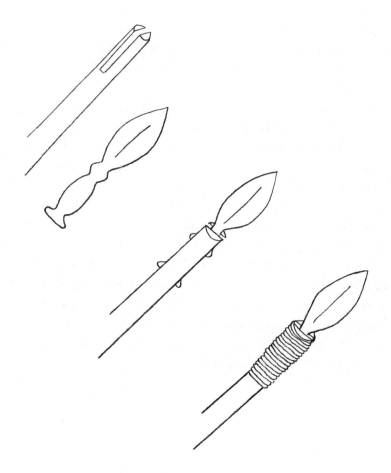

Figure 2.1 *Making a Light Spear*

THROWING THE LIGHT SPEAR

Throwing a spear such as the one described on the previous page requires a strong arm but a light touch. The grip therefore should be firm but not tight.

As the spear is raised to shoulder level, the wrist is bent so that the hand is palm up and the spear is parallel to the ground. The shaft of the spear runs across the heel of the hand and between the thumb and the first finger. All four fingers rest on top of the shaft while the thumb runs along the length of the shaft. The spear should be gripped at the balance point or slightly forward.

The throwing motion demands the coordination of the entire body and will require practice. For a right-handed person, the throwing motion begins with the right foot a step ahead of the left. The spear is gripped as described above and held parallel to the ground with the hand slightly ahead of the right shoulder. From this starting position, the left foot moves forward while the right hand is drawn back as it would be when throwing a football. The spear remains level or the point slightly elevated. As the left foot is touching down a step ahead of the right foot, the right hip and shoulder begin to rotate to the left. At this point the arm, hand, and spear are driven forward. Although this throwing motion is broken down here into steps, always remember that this is to be a smooth, fluid, and well timed motion.

Figure 2.2
Proper grip for throwing spear

Figure 2.3 - 2.7
Throwing motion for light spear

Figure 2.3 - 2.7 (continued)
Throwing motion for light spear

The accuracy of your throw will depend to a great extent on your release and follow through. The spear should feel as if it is rolling from your fingertips as it leaves your hand. This will ensure a light touch and will impart a spin which will help to keep the spear from wobbling in flight. The wrist should snap forward and the arm and shoulder should be fully extended in a straight line toward your target. Your left foot will now be your forward foot and you should finish in a deep forward stance. Proper release and follow through will give you the needed control over your throwing spear and will serve to guide it to its mark. As you will find, the spear is easy to throw. Practice is the key to polishing your technique and improving your strength and accuracy.

Although I generally throw at wooden targets, you may find that a bale of hay is easier to learn on and is less punishing to the spear.

THE SPEARTHROWER

The spearthrower in this instance does not refer to a person but to a device which was developed by primitive men perhaps 40,000 years ago. As men progressed and became more intelligent, their simple weapons (like the spear) became more refined. Weapons reached the point where the prevailing technology could no longer improve on them. No matter how well it might have been made, a spear with a stone head was still just that. It was at this point that men invented new ways to increase the power and the range of their hunting weapons. The next major advancement in weapon technology was the spearthrower.

The spearthrower is a very simple implement. Although it is not a weapon in itself, it launches the spear and increases its range and power. Made of wood, bone, or antler, spearthrowers are generally 12 to 16 inches long and can be either rod-like or somewhat long and flat in design. One end of the spearthrower is hooked or notched to receive the blunt end of the spear. At the other end of the spearthrower, there may be some type of handle or even a cord which goes through the spearthrower and loops around the thrower's wrist. To make a spearthrower is really quite easy; to use a spearthrower effectively requires considerable practice.

MAKING A SPEARTHROWER

A simple and authentic spearthrower can be made in a matter of minutes. Go into the woods or you own backyard and cut a forked branch at its base from a tree. At least one of the two branches must be straight for 12 to 16 inches for the length and 1/2 inch to 1 inch for the diameter. Trim the branch so that the straightest limb is approximately sixteen inches long and the other is one inch long. The short branch should be trimmed down to a stout point that will fit flush with the butt end of the spear. This then is your basic spearthrower: you may shorten or otherwise alter it as you learn to use it.

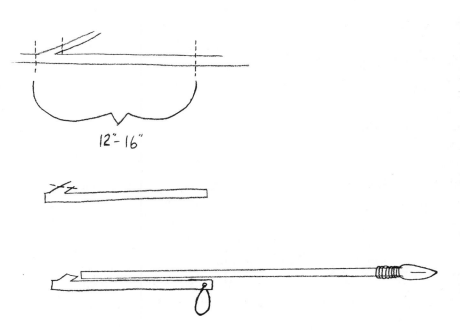

Figure 2.8 *Making a spearthrower from a forked branch*

USING A SPEARTHROWER

I assume you have fashioned a spearthrower to the previous specifications and have the spear ready. Next, find a large open area in which to practice. Begin by placing the blunt end of the spear into the notched or hooked end of the spearthrower. If you are right-handed, raise the spear and spearthrower using both hands to your right shoulder, so that the spear rests on top of the spearthrower. Throughout the throw, the left hand will balance and guide the spear while the right hand provides the thrust and power. How you will hold or grip the handle end of the spearthrower will be determined by its size and design. You should experiment with the grip until you find what works best for you. You may find it helpful to maintain contact on the spear with your right thumb and index finger throughout the throwing motion up to the point of release.

THE THROWING MOTION

Begin the throwing motion with the right foot a step ahead of the left and the spearthrower and spear held as described above at shoulder level. As the left foot starts forward toward the target, the right hand is drawn back behind the right shoulder. As the left foot is setting down a step ahead of the right foot, the forward motion of the spear begins. The spearthrower pulls the spear toward the target. As the wrist snaps forward at the end of the motion, the spearthrower, acting as an extension of the arm, launches the spear into the air with tremendous velocity and power.

Figure 2.9 - 2.14
Throwing motion for light spear with spearthrower

Figure 2.9 - 2.14 (continued)
Throwing motion for light spear with spearthrower

This little device called the spearthrower was the first major advancement of the spear in hundreds of thousands of years. The spearthrower apparently caught on rather quickly as it has been found in prehistoric sites around the world. The oldest surviving spearthrowers appear to be from northern Europe and are made from reindeer antlers. In the western hemisphere, the spearthrower is often referred to as the "altalt". In Australia (which is one of the few places left on earth where the spearthrower is still used), the Aborigines call it the "womera".

As I mentioned earlier, although the throwing spear is declining as a necessary primitive weapon, its use for sport is rapidly growing. Scout camps, outdoor clubs, and other groups are competing with spears across the nation. Although there are no universally set standards governing the sport, it is quite simple to develop your own regulations for competition. Standards governing throwing distance, targets, and spear design can be created to suit your situation.

I should mention here that the throwing spear (along with some of the other weapons included in this book) has also been gaining popularity as a hunting weapon. This is a very interesting and often controversial topic in some areas of the country. If you are at all interested in this aspect of the sport, you should be certain to check with your state's wildlife agency. State laws vary widely as to which animals may be hunted and what weapons are acceptable to use while hunting.

The spear has a very interesting history and has played an important role in the development of early mankind around the world. It is representative of a time when men's needs were less complex. Perhaps the recently renewed interest in the throwing spear and other basic weapons of early men by outdoor clubs, scouting organizations, hunters, and others is an attempt to escape, if only briefly, to a more basic time.

3.
THROWING KNIVES

At present, the most popular of all throwing weapons is probably the knife, although this has not always been the case. The first knives were made of stone such as flint or chert, and they were used as cutting instruments. These Stone Age knives were mainly used to skin and to butcher animals and were seldom thrown as weapons. When metals such as bronze and later iron were developed, knives were fashioned which were lighter, stronger, and more durable. This is when men began knife throwing as we know it today.

The fascination of throwing knives is hard to explain, but if you give a young boy a knife, sooner or later he is going to try to throw it. We have probably all seen knives thrown on television or at the movies or even perhaps in person at a circus. Most of us in fact have probably tried our hand at throwing a knife at one time or another. Unless you were lucky enough to have some proper instruction, chances are that your attempts met with little success. If that was the case, take heart. You are about to see that it is not really that hard to become a proficient knife thrower once you learn the basic fundamentals.

SELECTING A KNIFE

The first step to becoming a proficient thrower is to select a good knife. There are all kinds of knives and most knives can be thrown. However, some knives undoubtedly perform better than others. The very best throwing knives are usually the high quality knives which are designed specifically for throwing. Many so-called throwing knives however are often poorly made and do not perform as well as a good hunting knife or a butcher knife.

The main factors to consider when selecting a knife for throwing are: durability, length, weight, and balance. As for durability, the knife should be made of high quality steel. The best throwing knives are made from steel that is not so brittle that it will snap nor is it so thin and soft that it will bend. The handles, as well as the hilt of the knife, should be small and well secured or absent entirely. As far as the length of the knife is concerned, I find anywhere from 8-15 inches is acceptable and 11-13 is preferable. The length of the knife determines to a great extent your control over it. If a knife is too short, it may spin too fast. But a long knife can be awkward. The weight of a knife is also an important factor. A light knife will often not penetrate your target consistently, and one that is too heavy will hinder your ability to throw correctly. Find a knife which feels comfortable in your hand and seems to be in good proportion to its length. The last major factor to consider in looking for a knife to throw is balance. Stay away from knives which have excessively heavy handles or which otherwise feel awkward. The point of balance however does not have to be at the exact center of the knife for it to be well balanced. Generally, a knife which is heavier in the handle is thrown by the blade and a knife which is blade heavy is thrown from the handle. Some throwing knives are designed so that they can be thrown equally well from the handle or the blade.

Before you begin throwing your knife, I feel it is important to mention a few **safety** precautions. The first step is to find a suitable place to throw. An ideal place is an open, grassy area where the likelihood of injury to people, pets, or private property is minimal. Secondly, an important thing to remember about throwing knives is that they can ricochet or even bounce straight back. **Do not stand too close to your target.** As for targets, a crosscut circle from a large tree is best. If a crosscut section is not readily available, large, heavy boards of a soft type of wood are a good second choice. Plywood is often hard to penetrate and therefore can be dangerous to beginning throwers. Let common sense be your guide where safety is concerned. If a situation appears unsafe, then correct it before proceeding.

THROWING A KNIFE

The main problem most people have when first learning to throw a knife is consistency. Many people can stick the knife in the target two or three times out of ten, but they never really improve. Since the flight pattern of a knife is end over end, it is necessary that the knife hits the target at just the right point in its rotation time after time. To achieve this kind of control requires a consistent throwing action. I will teach you the proper grip, stances, throwing motions, and other factors which will enable you to develop this consistency.

THE GRIP

The first fundamental of knife throwing is the proper grip. As I mentioned earlier, a knife may be thrown by gripping either the handle or the blade depending on the knife. When throwing a knife by the handle, the hand position looks much the same as it would if you were pulling hard on a one inch thick rope. The wrist is bent forward, the fingers are angled back, and the thumb may be either closed around the handle or running along the top edge of the handle. The grip must be firm, but not too tight, and must be maintained throughout the entire throwing motion until the knife is released.

Gripping a knife by the blade is somewhat different. A knife which is designed to be thrown by the blade will usually have only one sharp edge. A knife such as this will be held flat to the ground with the sharp edge away from the hand. The fingers should be angled back with the flat of the fingertips against the bottom side of the blade and the thumb on top. This grip is also firm and must be maintained throughout the entire throwing motion until the moment of release.

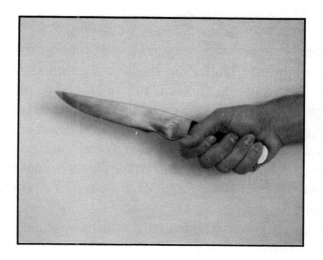

Figure 3.1
*Proper grip for knife thrown by
handle*

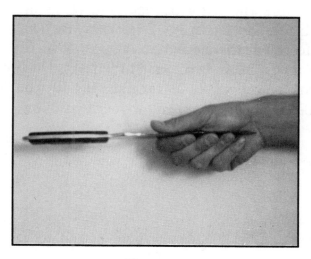

Figure 3.2
*Proper grip for knife thrown by
blade*

THROWING DISTANCE

Whether your knife was designed to be thrown by the handle or by the blade, the basic fundamentals as to the stance, the throwing motion, the release, and the follow through will be much the same. The main difference is that the spinning or turning action as well as the throwing distances will vary. A knife thrown by the handle must make at least one full turn in order to strike the target point first. A knife thrown by the blade needs only a half of a turn to strike the board point first.

There are simply too many factors to consider for me to tell you an ideal distance to stand from the target. With a few suggestions, you will find your correct distance easily enough by trial and error. If you have a knife to be thrown by the handle, find a spot 15-17 feet from your target and mark it. This is the approximate distance for one full turn of the average knife when thrown properly. If your knife is thrown by the blade, pick a spot 11-12 feet away for a half a turn or 20-21 feet away for one and a half turns. I will elaborate on how to adjust these distances a little later. Once you have paced off your distance and marked it, grip your knife as described above and prepare for your first throw.

THE THROWING MOTION

You are about to find that the motion of throwing a knife is very similar to that of a pitcher throwing a baseball. With the exception of the wrist action it may be helpful to keep this comparison in mind. Assuming that you are throwing right-handed, begin by placing your right foot a step ahead of your left foot and on top of your mark. The throwing motion begins with the knife in the right hand being drawn back behind your head as the left foot moves forward toward your target. As your weight shifts forward, and your left foot touches down, the right arm and shoulder drive the knife toward the target. It is important that your wrist does not snap forward at the moment of release, but that the knife just slips from your hand at the precise moment of alignment.

Now if the knife stuck in the target point on your first throw, and you feel that your throwing motion was correct, then congratulations! If your first throw was not successful, and you feel that your throwing motion was good, do not worry. Keep in mind not to snap your wrist and try it again. This time watch to see how the knife strikes the target. If the knife hits the target flat, with the point upward, this means that it did not complete turning in time. Take one step backward and try again. If however your knife hit flat against the board with the point down, this means you are probably too far from the target. Take one step forward. By this method of trial and error, you will soon find your ideal distance.

Figure 3.3 - 3.8
Author demonstrating throwing motion for knife

Figure 3.3 - 3.8 (continued)
Author demonstrating throwing motion for knife

Once you begin sticking the knife consistently in the target, you may want to improve your accuracy and increase your distance. As far as accuracy is concerned, the release and follow through are the key factors. As I mentioned earlier, the knife must slip smoothly from your hand. The wrist must not snap forward, and the throwing hand and arm should extend directly toward your target. Throwing knives is somewhat like shooting free-throws in basketball or hitting golf balls. The movement is the same time after time, and the more that you practice, the better you get.

As your accuracy begins to improve you will soon want to increase your throwing distances. Here again there are many variables to consider, but as a general rule, you will find that your knife will complete another full turn at 8 to 10 feet beyond your original mark. If your original mark was 16 feet for one turn, it should be 24 to 26 feet for two turns, and then another 8 to 10 feet beyond that for three turns. The throwing motion will remain exactly the same. Your throwing distance will be limited only by the strength of your arm and your ability to control the knife.

ADVANCED METHODS

Once you feel that you have mastered the basic throw, you may want to experiment with a few advanced techniques which will enable you to throw from distances between full turns of the knife. One method to achieve this is to increase or decrease your wrist action. Increasing your wrist action at the moment of release will increase the speed at which the knife spins or turns through the air. By decreasing this wrist action, you will slow the spinning down. By experimenting in this way, you will be able to cover the intermediate distances between full turns of the knife. To master this will require many additional hours of practice and is considered to be very advanced knife throwing. The other alternative is to acquire a knife which can be thrown equally well by the blade or by the handle. By being able to grip the knife by either the handle or the blade, you can cover the distances of one half turn, one full turn, 1 and 1/2 turns, two turns, and so on without having to alter your wrist action or throwing motion.

If knife throwing really appeals to you, then you are not alone. All over the country there are people throwing knives and other weapons in competition or just for fun. There may be Buckskinner clubs, Blackpowder clubs, knife-throwing organizations, or other similar groups in your area. Whether you choose to join one of these organizations or simply throw in your own backyard, I am sure you will find that the sport of knife throwing provides an interesting challenge and hours of fun.

4.
THROWING
AXES AND TOMAHAWKS

Many thousands of years ago, men began to discover that a stone when well attached to the end of a short stick proved be quite an effective weapon. Compared to a wooden club, a stone axe was much more effective as a tool and as a weapon. Leverage and striking power were both increased and even these Stone Age axes were deadly when thrown with skill. In the thousands of years that men carried stone axes, many lives were probably saved and many more lives were probably taken by the swinging and the throwing of such an axe.

In later years, when bronze and iron were developed, weapons including axe heads were among the first metal implements made. Metal axes could be made lighter, stronger, and more durable than stone ones thus making them easier to wield and to throw. These bronze weapons were being made throughout the Middle East and Greece as far back as 3000 B.C. The iron weapons (which were much better weapons than the bronze ones) were first developed about two thousand years later in the same part of the world. It did not take long for these metal weapons to spread into the surrounding areas. Many warriors throughout Europe and Asia down through the centuries carried battleaxes into war. Many stories of these warriors' encounters and the role that the battleaxes played in these encounters have been told and retold down through the ages.

While all this was taking place in Europe, Asia, and North Africa, the Indians in North and South America were still living in the Stone Age.

It is thought that the Vikings were the first people to introduce iron implements to the North American Indians somewhere around 1000 A.D. Native Americans however did not really gain access to iron axes and other tools until much later when in the sixteenth century European trappers and traders began dealing with them.

Early traders found that the stone axes and warclubs played an important part in Indian culture. The traders were very eager to supply the Indians with iron hatchets in exchange for furs. The Indians were equally anxious to obtain the iron tomahawks which were highly prized and quickly circulated throughout New England and other areas where the fur trade flourished. To the Indians, the tomahawk functioned as a tool, as a weapon, and as a ceremonial object and they were very adept in its use.

As the white men soon found out, the iron tomahawk proved to be a very effective weapon in the hand to hand combat which was often prevalent in the early exploration and settlement of North America. Because the tomahawk was such an effective weapon as well as a practical tool, it was often used by many of the white explorers, trappers, and military men up through the nineteenth century. Daniel Boone, members of the Lewis and Clark expedition, and many early British and American troops were among the many white men who choose to carry a tomahawk.

In modern times, tomahawks and axes are still popular. They are being thrown throughout North America and elsewhere as a means of sport and recreation. Competitive axe throwing has always been common among lumberjacks; the tomahawk or hatchet throw is a popular activity with many outdoorsmen and their organizations. Depending on where you live, there may be groups in your area with names like "Buckskinners", "Mountain Men", or "Black Powder Clubs" which hold annual meets or rendezvous. These rendezvous (gatherings) often try to recreate the atmosphere of the mountainmen in the first half of the nineteenth century, both in the way that they dress and in their activities. It is not at all uncommon to see organized competitions in knife, spear, and tomahawk throwing at these meetings, along with blackpowder weapons of the historic period that they are trying to recapture. Whether you join one of these organizations or throw in your own backyard, you will find that throwing a tomahawk or axe is a developed skill which can bring you many hours of fun as well as add to your outdoor experience.

Just as in dealing with other weapons, precautions must be observed when throwing tomahawks and axes. I often go out to the desert or the mountains around my home in Las Vegas to throw weapons. This way there isn't any danger of any harm coming to people or animals while I do my throwing. Many times I have overthrown my target and I am glad my tomahawk did not end up in anyone's backyard. Be sure you have plenty of space and also a target that will stop a tomahawk. A couple of other things to watch out for are: 1) the tomahawk or axe head slipping from the handle; 2) wild ricochets; 3) weapons bouncing straight back at you. **Keep in mind that tomahawks are very effective and dangerous weapons. Caution must be observed when handling these weapons.**

CHOOSING YOUR WEAPON

One reason the tomahawk is a very effective weapon is that it is relatively easy to throw and quite deadly when thrown. There have been many different types of tomahawks down through the centuries. Many of these were better suited for ceremonial purposes rather than for actual combat or throwing. There are a few things to look for when you select a tomahawk or axe for throwing. First of all, the tomahawk or axe that you choose must be sturdy. The weapon will undergo considerable punishment as you learn to throw it correctly. Be sure that the handle is strong and can be well secured to the tomahawk or axe head. Since all tomahawks and axes are top heavy, balance is not a critical factor to consider. Choose a weapon which is not too heavy for you to throw and that feels comfortable in your hand. Whether you select a tomahawk, a hatchet, or a small axe, the basic fundamentals for throwing will be the same.

THROWING DISTANCE

The tomahawk being somewhat heavy is generally thrown at a distance which will allow it to make just one complete turn before striking the target. However, people with strong arms can throw the tomahawk from greater distances and still maintain enough control to be accurate. As a beginner, you will find that your distance from the target will vary depending upon such factors as the length and weight of your tomahawk or axe as well as your own size and strength. Other factors in your throwing motion (such as wrist action) will affect the rate that your tomahawk spins which will in turn affect your throwing distance. You should work to become proficient at a distance of a single rotation before moving on to two or three turns.

For your first throw, begin at a distance of about 18-20 feet from your target. I will discuss adjusting your throwing distance once you have learned the fundamentals of throwing a tomahawk.

THE GRIP

Throwing a tomahawk correctly requires that you begin with a good grip.

Simply grip the tomahawk or hatchet for throwing as if you were chopping wood with it. As with throwing a knife, the wrist action at the moment of release will be minimal, and the tomahawk should slip easily from your hand. Too much wrist action may cause you to flip the tomahawk from your hand, resulting in a weak, erratic throw.

Figure 4.1
*Tomahawk hits the mark at proper angle
of 45 degrees*

Figure 4.2
Proper grip for tomahawk

THROWING MOTION

The throwing motion for a tomahawk is the same basic overhand throwing motion used to throw rocks, baseballs, knives, and other objects, with just a few exceptions. Keep in mind that the emphasis should be on control, not power, since the tomahawk does not need to be thrown extremely hard. Assuming you are right-handed, begin with your right foot a step ahead of your left foot. The tomahawk should be held either in front of you or at your right side. The throwing motion begins with the tomahawk being drawn back behind your right shoulder as your left foot moves toward a deep front stance. As your left foot is setting down firmly in front of you, the forward motion of the tomahawk begins. You should have the feeling that the whole right side of your body, your shoulder, and your right arm are pulling the tomahawk forward and toward the target. Knowing the exact moment at which to release the tomahawk will be instinctive and will improve with practice. It is important that the tomahawk slips easily from your hand and that your arm follows through in a direct line toward your mark. Good release and follow-through will improve your accuracy and help to eliminate any wobbling or erratic flight of the tomahawk.

Figure 4.3 - 4.8
Author demonstrating throwing motion for tomahawk

Figure 4.3 - 4.8 (continued)
Author demonstrating throwing motion for tomahawk

Ideally, the tomahawk should stick into the board with the handle pointing down at an angle of 45 degrees to the target face. If your first throw was successful, mark that distance and continue developing and improving your throwing motion. If however you were unsuccessful, throw the tomahawk again and watch to see how it strikes the board. When the tomahawk strikes the board on the top edge or the backside of the weapon's head, instead of the cutting edge, then the tomahawk has rotated slightly over one full turn. Taking one step closer to your target will generally correct this. If your weapon's handle strikes the target before the cutting edge, then the tomahawk has not completed one full rotation. One step further away from your target will usually be enough to improve your results. Assuming that your throwing motion is correct and consistent, you should soon be able to determine your own correct distance through this trial and error process.

Once you have mastered the basic throw, or single rotation, you may wish to increase your distance from the target. The throwing motion remains the same, but the tomahawk will need to make two or more rotations to cover the added distance. Generally you should allow another 12-15 feet for each additional turn of the tomahawk. Again, watch the weapon in flight and use the trial and error process to narrow down your own correct distance.

I hope that the ideas and fundamentals presented here have stimulated your interest in throwing tomahawks and axes. What I have presented here is fairly basic, but it is what you must know if you wish to get started in this sport. You may eventually learn to throw a tomahawk or axe held backwards or underhanded or even learn to throw a double edged weapon. These are just progressions once you have learned the basic fundamentals. Whether or not you decide to become an expert, I think you will find tomahawk and axe throwing to be a very challenging sport. Be careful, be safe, and have fun.

5.
THE SHURIKEN

The shuriken (throwing star) is a weapon which is believed to have been developed in China, perhaps as long ago as a thousand years. Made of metal and ranging in size from two to five inches in diameter and 1/16th to 1/8th of an inch in thickness, the shuriken is a flat, multi-pointed, star-shaped weapon designed for throwing. The shuriken was a later development as far as simple weapons were concerned. This is due to the fact that it lacked the killing power of the spear, the sword, the bow, and other weapons of the time. Additionally, unlike a knife or an axe, it was not very effective as a hand held weapon.

Although the shuriken was not a primary weapon in major battles, it was still considered a very effective weapon. When thrown with skill and power, the shuriken was very accurate and could cause serious and disabling wounds. The shurikens were also easy to conceal, and unlike a knife or an axe, could be thrown without regard to the distance or the number of turns the weapon made before reaching its mark. As a weapon, shurikens were suited to guerrilla type warfare and self-defense. It was for these reasons that shurikens were much favored by the Ninja warriors of Japan many years later. The Ninjas were an elite group of warriors who used almost mystical powers to perform special missions which required great skill and cunning.

In recent years as the American public has become more exposed to the world of Oriental martial arts, the shuriken is experiencing a renewed popularity and some notoriety. Although many martial art students are interested mainly in the unarmed forms and techniques, many are also interested in Oriental weapons. Bow staffs, nunchakus, sais, and shurikens are turning up almost everywhere. I say almost everywhere because the possession and/or use of the shuriken is prohibited by law in some states and communities. Find out what your state and local laws are before attempting to buy or use shurikens. If shurikens are illegal in your area, do not break the law, but concentrate on other chapters of this book. In spite of or maybe because of this notoriety, the shuriken has become one of the most popular of the Oriental weapons. Millions have been sold in the United States recently. Despite this great interest, very little has been written concerning this weapon. Many people are in the dark as to the proper way to throw a shuriken.

In researching this weapon, I found it interesting that when asking ten different "experts" the proper way to hold and to throw a shuriken, I would get ten different answers. The reasons for this are many and vary from tradition to ignorance. However, if your goal is to throw a shuriken with maximum accuracy, versatility, and power, from any distance, then the possibilities are greatly reduced. I have included two different throwing motions which when learned together will make you a very adept and versatile shuriken thrower. The two methods are the overhand throwing motion and the horizontal throwing motion. The first step though is selecting the proper shuriken or throwing star.

Figure 5.1
Different types of shurikens in hanging target

SELECTING A SHURIKEN

Selecting a good shuriken can often be a problem for a beginner. As with selecting a good throwing knife, a shuriken should be made of flexible, high quality steel. It should also have sufficient weight for ease of handling and penetration into your target. Shurikens come in all shapes, weights, and sizes; some designs perform better than others. The best shurikens I have found for overall performance are four to eight pointed, stainless steel stars, and are approximately four inches in diameter and 1/16th of an inch thick. Assuming they are legal in your area, it should not be hard to find these stars in local martial art supply stores or karate studios. If you have any trouble finding throwing stars in your area, check within the pages of most any martial arts magazine and you will find them advertised. Now that you have selected one or more suitable shurikens, there is one more important aspect to discuss. **This aspect is safety.**

Safety is one factor which must not be taken lightly. Shurikens were designed to be weapons and like any other weapon can be dangerous if not handled correctly. Most important of all, you must have a **safe** place to throw. It is not uncommon especially when you first learn to throw a shuriken for the weapon to ricochet off your target or even miss it completely. You must have an area large enough so that there is no danger or injury to people, pets, or property due to an errant throw. Do not allow people to come between you and your target or even near your target when you are throwing your shuriken. Finally, a good target will improve your performance and contribute to your safety. A large, flat surface of soft wood makes the best target for shurikens.

THROWING A SHURIKEN

Having selected your shuriken and a suitable place to throw, the fun now begins. As I have mentioned, I will be describing two different throwing motions for the shuriken, the overhand and the horizontal. Although these two methods are quite different, the basic way to grip or hold the shuriken is nearly the same for both.

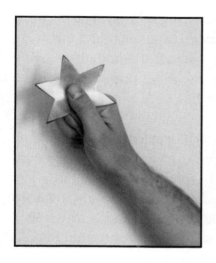 

Figure 5.2
*Proper grip for shuriken
thrown overhand*

Figure 5.3
*Proper grip for shuriken
thrown horizontally*

THE GRIP

The best way to hold a shuriken is shown in figures **5. 2.** and **5.3.** The shuriken is held firmly between the thumb and the outside of the index finger with the hand closed. The hand is held so that the shuriken is either perpendicular or horizontal to the ground, depending on which throwing motion you intend to use. Other grips are sometimes used, but this grip is the safest, most dependable, and can be used with all shurikens.

THE OVERHAND THROWING MOTION

Of all the throwing motions I have encountered for the shuriken, I find the overhand throwing motion to be the most powerful and the easiest to master. The overhand throwing motion is also as accurate as any other method of throwing shurikens. The motion of the overhand throw is much the same as the action that a pitcher uses when throwing a fastball.

Assuming you are throwing right-handed, begin by holding the shuriken as described above, with your right foot forward and your shoulders and hips square to the target. The throwing motion begins with the left foot moving forward toward your target as the shuriken in your hand is drawn back slightly behind your right ear and above your shoulder. As the left foot touches down, a step ahead of your right foot, the right shoulder moves forward, pulling your arm, hand, and shuriken toward the target. The shuriken should slip smoothly from between your thumb and index finger as the wrist snaps forward. The point at which you release the shuriken will be determined by your distance from the target. It will generally be at or slightly above eye level. Although stepping into the throw as described above is considered optional, I feel it is to your advantage. Stepping into the throw will only not increase your power and possible throwing distance, but will improve your timing and rhythm as well.

Figure 5.4 - 5.7
*Author demonstrating overhand throwing motion for
shuriken*

THE HORIZONTAL THROWING MOTION

The horizontal throwing motion appears to be the more traditional and more common method of throwing a shuriken. As with the overhand throwing motion, the horizontal throwing motion allows for a high degree of control and accuracy, even though it is less powerful than the overhand throw. Also, if the overhand throwing motion can be compared to pitching a baseball, then the horizontal throwing motion can be likened to tossing a frisbee.

Again assuming that you are throwing right-handed, the horizontal throw begins with the right foot forward and pointed at the target. The left foot is turned perpendicular or at a 90 degree angle to the line of your front foot. Both knees should be bent, and the majority of your body weight is centered comfortably over your back foot. The throwing

Figure 5.8 - 5.10
Author demonstrating horizontal throwing motion for shurikens

Figure 5.8 - 5.10 (continued)
*Author demonstrating horizontal throwing motion for
shurikens*

motion begins with the shuriken being drawn back across the
front of your body to a position just below your left ribs. The
forward motion starts with your body weight shifting forward
while at the same time the right arm is pulling your hand and
the shuriken in a direct line toward the target. The shuriken
is released with a smooth, whip like action at approximately
chest height. It will usually require a fair amount of practice
to develop the timing, the coordination, and the rhythm
necessary to become skilled in this method of throwing
shurikens. I believe you will find that the practice pays off
in the satisfaction you will receive from watching the shuriken
as it floats, spins, curves, and then sinks into your target.

These then are the two methods which I recommend for throwing the shuriken. When they are learned and practiced together, these methods will enable you to become quite skilled with the weapon. Although I feel these are the most accurate and powerful methods of throwing a shuriken, there are other ways as well. Experimenting with these other ways may prove both interesting and entertaining.

6.
BOOMERANGS

When you hear the word boomerang, what thoughts first come into your mind? Like many people, you probably see images of Australian Aborigines throwing the small sickle-shaped sticks at kangaroos. You might wonder how in the world they ever killed anything with such a weapon. You might wonder also how a weapon which appears so simple can behave so mysteriously. These are often the first and only thoughts that people have about boomerangs. There is much more however to the boomerang story.

BOOMERANG TYPES

The boomerang is perhaps the most mysterious and interesting of all the primitive weapons ever created by man. What may be just as mysterious however as the boomerang's flight characteristics is its true origins. This is due in part to the fact that there are many different types of boomerangs found in many different places throughout the world. For the sake of simplicity, boomerangs are generally classified as either returning or non-returning boomerangs. The non-returning boomerangs are by far the most common type of boomerang or throw-stick used by primitive people both for hunting and for warfare. The returning boomerangs on the other hand were very likely first developed by the Aborigines of Australia as a toy or possibly as a weapon for hunting birds.

Even though the non-returning boomerang was in the past the most widely used of the two boomerangs, it is the returning boomerang of Australia which has received the most modern attention. Within the past few decades, interest in both types of boomerangs has grown steadily. The making, the throwing, and the study of the aerodynamic properties of boomerangs has proven to be an interesting project for everyone from Boy Scouts to physics students and aerospace engineers.

Figure 6.1
Boomerangs are fun for everyone

HISTORY OF BOOMERANGS

As I mentioned earlier, the real mystery of the boomerang is not so much how it flies but where it originated. This is a controversial question which may never be answered for certain. One reason for this is that the boomerangs are very primitive weapons and the earliest ones were most certainly made of wood and long ago deteriorated. It is interesting to note that the boomerangs have been found in ancient Egyptian tombs and have also been depicted in African rock paintings dating back perhaps 8 or 9 thousand years ago. It is very probable that the boomerangs were independently developed since they seem to have appeared in many early cultures throughout the world. It is also very possible that the boomerang is older than we know and that it was carried by migrating primitive men as they wandered throughout the continents. Whatever the case may be, flat, crescent shaped throwing sticks have been found in India, Borneo, Egypt, Ethiopia, southwestern United States, Australia, and many other locations around the world.

It is the Aborigines of Australia which seem to make the greatest use of the boomerang these days. Their use of the boomerang is certainly the most well documented. The word boomerang itself is derived from native Australian language. Significantly, there are only a few areas of Australia where the boomerang appears not to have been used by the native people.

THE NON-RETURNING BOOMERANGS

In Australia as elsewhere, the most widespread and common boomerang used has been the non-returning boomerang. This boomerang is generally about 3 feet long, 2 to 3 inches wide, and 1/4 to 1/2 inch thick. It is usually either flat on the bottom surface and convex on the top or bi-convex in cross section. The shape of these non-returning boomerangs varies greatly. Some boomerangs are widely angled or they can be almost straight. Other boomerangs are gently curved and some in certain parts of Australia are hooked at one end. The cross sectional design of the non-returning boomerang provides it with an aerodynamic lift which enables it to fly much farther and more accurately than an ordinary stick. A boomerang of this type can fly from 50 to 150 yards, depending on its design and the ability of the thrower. The non-returning boomerang is a perfect weapon for the type of flat, open country predominant in Australia. Since the boomerang spins in a horizontal plane, it can fly quite close to the ground and cut a wide path through the air. These boomerangs have been used by the Aborigines of Australia and other primitive people throughout the world for hunting and for battle. They are truly lethal weapons.

MAKING A NON-RETURNING BOOMERANG

If you would like to make and throw a non-returning boomerang, it should prove to be an interesting project. The Aborigines of Australia often use the wood of acacia trees or shrubs and shape the boomerang with whatever stone or metal tools are available. Depending on the materials and tools you have available, it should be somewhat easier for you. If you have a small hand saw or a saber saw, a rasp, and a sanding block, you can make a very good boomerang in a short period of time.

The first step in constructing a boomerang is to select a dense piece of wood, preferably a high quality plywood or a hardwood board 3/8th of an inch thick. Using **figure 6.2** on the following page as a guide, create your own boomerang design. Next trace your design onto the wood and then using your saw, cut the boomerang's shape from the board. Using a rasp, begin shaping the boomerang so that it appears convex (outwardly curved) on both the top and the bottom surfaces. As your boomerang begins to take shape, read up to the throwing instructions and begin test flying your boomerang. Remember that your boomerang may curve somewhat right or it may curve somewhat left. It will seldom fly perfectly straight: do not expect it perform that way. If your boomerang sinks quickly, you can give it more lift by bevel cutting the undersides of the wingtips or by flattening slightly the entire underside of the boomerang. If the boomerang climbs too fast, reduce the lift by reversing this process.

Finally, sanding and polishing your boomerang or throwstick will help to enhance its throwing qualities and protect the wood.

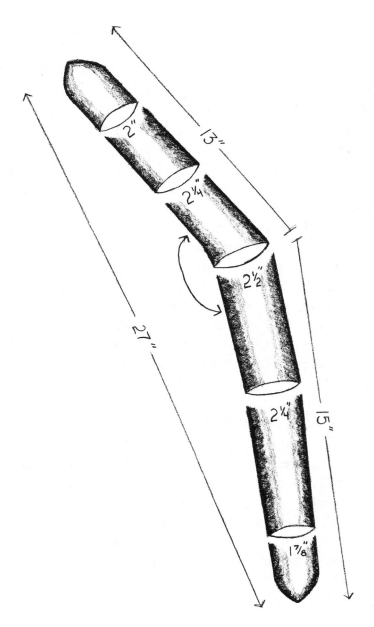

Figure 6.2 *Making a non-returning boomerang*

If you would like to make a more authentic boomerang, try cutting a sapling or a tree branch of an appropriate size and shape from almost any species of hardwood. Carving a boomerang from such a branch or sapling with a pocket knife can be a real challenge if you have the time and the inclination. The boomerang design on the preceding page will provide you with a guideline for making your own non-returning boomerang. You may find as I do that half the fun of these weapons is in the designing, building, and test flying of your own creations.

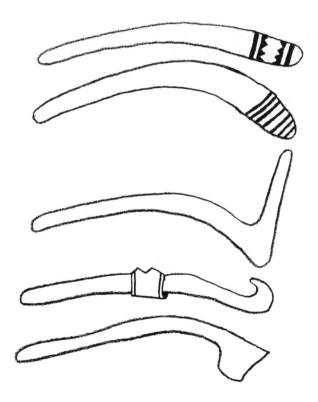

Figure 6.3 *Different types of non-returning boomerangs*

THROWING A NON-RETURNING BOOMERANG

Once you have designed and fashioned a non-returning boomerang, you'll hopefully be anxious to test fly your own weapon. It is important to remember that a boomerang can be a **dangerous weapon.** Find a large open meadow or an empty fairway on a golf course. It must be a large open area free of people and pets. It is unlikely but possible that your boomerang may fly 150 yards on your first throw. It may hook to the right or to the left and only you are responsible for where it may land.

Like throwing a returning boomerang, throwing a non-returning boomerang is a unique experience. A well thrown boomerang spinning through space and whipping the air while it gently curves or rises can be an awesome and beautiful sight. The throwing technique for boomerangs is not difficult to learn but requires a fair amount of practice to perfect.

THE GRIP

The design or shape of your boomerang will help determine which end to grip. If your boomerang is flat on one surface and convex on another, then the convex side should face toward your body with the flat side facing outward. If your boomerang is biconvex in cross section, then experiment to see which end produces the best results. The curve of the boomerang generally points forward as you grip the weapon, although this is open for experimentation. It is important to grip the boomerang firmly and as close to the end as possible to impart the necessary spin upon release.

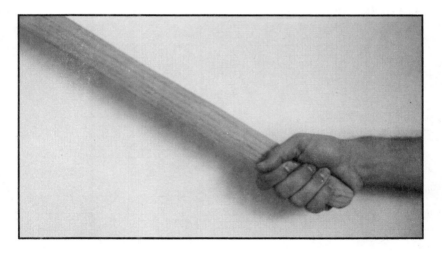

Figure 6.4
Proper grip for non-returning boomerang

THE THROWING MOTION

The throwing motion for the non-returning boomerang is somewhat like the motion used to skip a flat rock across a pond or to throw a baseball sidearm. If you are throwing right-handed, start with your right foot forward. Face the direction you are throwing toward and step forward with the left foot while drawing the boomerang well behind your head and right shoulder. As the left foot is touching down, the arm's forward motion begins. The right shoulder drops and the arm is turned so that the elbow and the hand are level to the ground with the forearm and hand both facing upward. As the arm sweeps forward, the wrist snaps releasing the boomerang at an angle between zero and 30 degrees to the horizon.

Figure 6.5 - 6.8
Author demonstrating throwing motion for non-returning boomerang

Figure 6.5 - 6.8 (continued)
*Author demonstrating throwing motion for non-returning
boomerang*

If your boomerang does not fly well, keep trying. It may be your throwing motion that needs work and not the boomerang. Experiment with your angle of release and the amount of spin upon release. If you determine there is a flaw in your boomerang, it is a good idea to have a rasp and a sanding block along with you to make the necessary adjustments. If this sounds like too much work and if you get tired of walking a hundred yards to retrieve your non-returning boomerang, you may find the returning boomerang more to your liking.

RETURNING BOOMERANGS

For thousands of years the non-returning boomerang has been the boomerangs most widely used by the Aborigines of Australia. Strangely enough, it is their toy the returning boomerang that has attracted so much recent attention. The traditional returning boomerang made by the natives of Australia is generally 12 to 20 inches long from tip to tip, 1 and 1/2 to 2 inches wide, and is curved or angled near its center at an angle of between 90 to 120 degrees. The arms of these boomerangs are from 1/4 to 1/2 of an inch thick and are either plano-convex or biconvex in cross section. The arms may or may not be slightly twisted in relation to each other. The design of the arms or wings of the boomerang provide a lifting force much like an airplane wing. The shape of the boomerang and its end over end spinning motion provides a gyroscope effect or a torquing action. The combination of these two physical forces impact on a well thrown boomerang and will cause it to return to the vicinity of the person throwing it.

Although it is said to be sometimes used for hunting birds, the Aborigines seem to consider the returning boomerang more a toy than a weapon. It is interesting that this toy developed by a primitive people should hold such a fascination for modern man as well. It does however fascinate us and within the past few decades boomerang clubs and organizations as well as International Competitions have been formed. High school and college physics classes, Scouting groups, and everyday people are finding it to be an interesting project to design, build and throw boomerangs.

MAKING A RETURNING BOOMERANG

Perhaps you have bought a boomerang in a sporting goods store or department store and thrown it until your arm ached. Yet it never once returned back to you. This is not unusual since there seem to be many more poorly made boomerangs in circulation than well made boomerangs. Unless you really know boomerangs, it can be very hard to tell a good one from a bad one without being able to test fly it. I have found that the best way to avoid getting a useless boomerang is to make one yourself. With a few tools, the right kind of wood, and a little bit of know how, you can make a boomerang which will return perfectly when thrown properly.

The first step in boomerang making is selecting the wood. The best material I have found for making boomerangs is high quality plywood such as marine or aircraft plywood 3/8th of an inch in thickness. This plywood is very durable and good to work with; however, it is expensive and comes generally in large sheets (4 by 8 feet in size). Fortunately, good boomerangs can also be fashioned from lesser quality plywood, tree branches, and boards of heavy wood.

Once you have selected the wood to be used for your boomerang, trace or draw the outline for the boomerang on the surface of the wood. Then get your saw. A saber saw will make cutting along the outline quick and easy. A handsaw and a little muscle will get the job done as well.

After you have cut the blank for your boomerang, prepare to shape it using a rasp and a sanding block. If you study the diagram (**6.8**) on page 84, you will see that the arms of the boomerang have a classic airfoil shape and a leading as well as a trailing edge. I want to point out that this diagram is for a right-handed boomerang and if you wish to make a left-handed boomerang, simply use the mirror image of this diagram. Next, clamp your boomerang in a vise and begin shaping the arms as shown in the diagram, with the leading edges rounded off and tapering back to the trailing edge. A slight bevel at the bottom of the leading edges (from the wingtip inward) for approximately 3 and 1/2 inches will provide your boomerang with added lift. When you feel satisfied with the shape of your boomerang, sand down any rough edges and give it a few test flights. If your boomerang performs well, you may wish to touch it up by decorating it, polishing it, or varnishing it. These finishing touches will not only help protect your boomerang but will add to its beauty in flight.

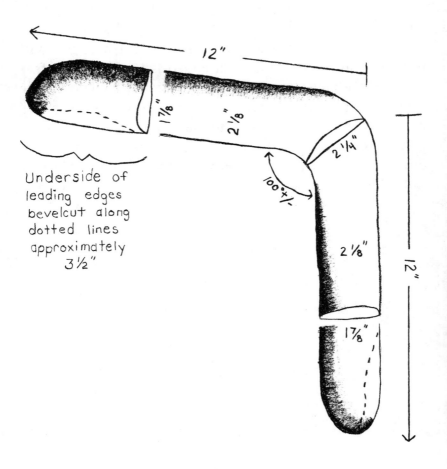

12"

1⅞"

2⅛"

2¼"

100°+/-

2⅛"

1⅞"

12"

Underside of
leading edges
bevelcut along
dotted lines
approximately
3½"

Figure 6.9 *Making a returning boomerang*

THROWING A RETURNING BOOMERANG

Now that you have your boomerang in hand, the next step is to find a safe place to throw. A calm day and a large grassy area where there is no danger of damaging personal property is the ideal situation. Boomerangs can be easily blown off course in a breeze or a gust of wind and can be carried surprisingly far. If you followed the design in this book for making your boomerang, its range may be 40 to 50 yards. The world's record is over 125 yards so allow yourself plenty of room.

THE GRIP

There are many different ways to grip or hold a boomerang. Feel free to experiment but keep in mind the following principles. First, the convex or curved surface of the boomerang must face inward or toward you and the flat surface outward. Secondly, you need to grip the boomerang so that you will get maximum spin upon release and still maintain good control throughout the throwing motion. I achieve this best by gripping 1 and 1/2 to 2 inches of the wingtip with the middle and index fingers curled around the boomerang. My thumb is pressing the boomerang into the upper corner of my palm.

The boomerang can be held at either wingtip so that the upper arm points either forward (most common grip position) or backward pointing over the shoulder.

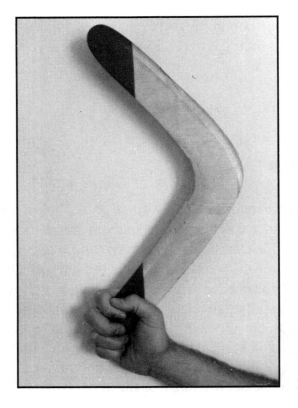

Figure 6.10
Proper grip for returning boomerang

THE THROWING MOTION

The throwing motion for a returning boomerang is the same overhand throwing motion used to throw rocks or baseballs. As the arm comes forward, the wrist snaps forward, releasing the boomerang straight ahead or slightly upward. At the moment of release, the boomerang should be inclined at an angle of approximately 60 degrees to the horizon. It is often helpful to aim at a distant object such as the top of a tree to provide consistency in your release and follow-through. If your boomerang is thrown properly, and is right-handed, the boomerang will fly straight ahead at first but soon will begin climbing skyward while it turns abruptly to the left. It will keep turning or bending to the left as it completes its circle and heads back to your vicinity. The boomerang may then land softly at your feet; it may hover over your head; or it may pass over you and circle back again. Boomerangs follow many different flight paths. If your boomerang climbs very rapidly and seems to float away, there is a good chance that you released the boomerang at an angle less than 60 degrees to the horizon. If your boomerang takes off well but does not seem to make its way back to you, then perhaps it was held too close to vertical upon release. If the boomerang takes off well and turns well, but seems to lose steam, then there is a good chance that you did not impart enough spin upon its release. Another important factor is the wind. You will seldom encounter a perfectly calm day, and the best way to deal with a breeze is to throw at an angle of approximately 45 degrees to the right of the wind direction.

The wind should be against your left cheek. Through a process of trial and error, and much practice, you will eventually find the groove. Your boomerang will return time and time again to your waiting hands.

Figure 6.11 - 6.14
Author demonstrating throwing motion for returning boomerang

Figure 6.11 - 6.14 (continued)
*Author demonstrating throwing motion for returning
boomerang*

Figure 6.15
Angle of boomerang at moment of release

If you thought throwing the boomerang was tricky, just wait until you try catching it. Catching boomerangs is not only tricky but can be slightly hazardous. **A few words of caution are in order.** First, if a boomerang is coming in fast or in a dive, do not try to catch it. Get out of the way. Also do not try to catch a boomerang anytime at face level. Wearing a heavy glove on your non-throwing hand will also give you some added protection when catching boomerangs. Lastly, rather than grabbing at the returning boomerang, try to trap it between the palms of your hands in a clapping motion. Be cautious at first until you get to know how your boomerang flies. Soon you will be catching it with the greatest of ease.

I think you will agree that boomerangs are truly fascinating devices and it is little wonder that they are becoming so popular. Whether you are looking for a new hobby or just an interesting and entertaining way to spend a Saturday afternoon, you might want to give boomeranging a try.

Figure 6.16

CLOSING

I hope that during the course of this book you have had the chance to experience the sensation that I described earlier. To experience the thrill of watching a perfectly returning boomerang or the sight and sound of a knife or tomahawk as it strikes its mark is very rewarding.

These sensations and skills are the ones that I sought out and found and have tried to pass on to you. I feel confident that armed with the knowledge in this book, the proper equipment, and the willingness to put in the necessary hours of practice, you can become very skillful with any or all of these weapons. Included in the following pages are some of the references that I found helpful in many ways. You may find them interesting and useful as well. Be safe, have fun, and remember that there is no substitute for practice.

REFERENCES

Adams, Andrew, Ninja, the Invisible Assassins. Burbank, California:
>   Ohara Publications, Inc., 1973.

Collins, Blackie, Knife Throwing, Sport, Survival, Defense. Knoxville, TN: Knife World.

Corish, Joseph J. III, "The Mystery of the Boomerang," Natural History, Vol. 65, 1956, pp. 242-245.

Davidson, D.S., "Australian Throwing Sticks, Throwing-Clubs, and Boomerangs," American Anthropologist, Vol. 38, 1936, pp. 76-100.

Diagram Group, Weapons, Weapons, An International Encyclopedia from 5000 B.C.to 2000 A.D..
>   New York: St. Martin's Press, 1980.

Hall, Stephens, "Boom in 'rangs Launches Old Toy into New Orbit,"
>   Smithsonian, June 1984, pp. 118-25.

Hayes, Stephen K., The Ninja and Their Secret Fighting Art. Tokyo, Japan: Charles E. Tuttle Co., 1981.

Hayes, Stephen K., Ninjutsu. Chicago, Illinois: Contemporary Books Inc., 1984.

Hayes, Stephen K., "Ninjutsu, Art of Stealth," Black Belt, August 1979, pp. 40-43.

Hess, Felix, "The Aerodynamics of Boomerangs," Scientific American, November 1968, pp. 124-136.

Hogg, O.F.G., Club to Cannon. London: Gerald Duckworth and Co. LTD.,1968.

Kubota, Takayuki, The Ninja Shuriken Manual. USA: I & I Sports Supply Co., 1985.

Lewis, Meriwether, Original Journals of the Lewis and Clark Expedition.
        Fd. Reuben Gold Thwaites, LL.D. 8 Vols. New York: Arno Press, 1969.

Mason, Bernard S., Boomerangs: How to Make and Throw Them. New York:
        Dover Publications, 1974.

McEvoy, Harry K. and Charles V. Gruzanski, Knife Throwing as a Modern Sport. Springfield, Illinois: Charles C. Thomas (Publisher), 1965.

McEvoy, Harry K., Knife Throwing, A Practical Guide. Tokyo, Japan:
Charles E. Tuttle Company, Inc., 1973.

McEvoy, Harry K., Knife Throwing in the Professional Style. Grand Rapids: The Tru-Bal Co., 1969.

Musgrove, Peter, "Many Happy Returns," New Scientists, January 24, 1974, pp. 186-189.

Nickel, Helmut, Warriors and Worthies. New York: Atheneum, 1969.

Parulski, George R. Jr., The Art of Karate Weapons. Chicago, Illinois: Contemporary Books, Inc., 1984.

Peterson, Harold L., American Indian Tomahawks. New York: Museum of the American Indian, 1965.

Peterson, Harold L., Daggers and Fighting Knives of the Western World.
New York: Walker and Company, 1968.

Prideaux, Tom, Cro-Magnon Man: The Emergence of Man. New York: Time-Life Books, 1973.

Ruhe, Benjamin, Boomerang. Washington, D.C.: Minner Press, 1982.

Russel, Carl P., Firearms,Traps and Tools of the Mountain Men. New York: Alfred A. Knopf, 1967.

Tunis, Edwin, Weapons, A Pictorial History. New York: Thomas Y. Crowell Co., 1954.

Walker, Jearl, "Boomerangs! How to Make Them and Also How They Fly,"
     Scientific American, March 1979, pp. 162-172.

"Weapons and Delivery Systems," Encyclopedia Britannica, 1981, vol. 19, pp. 680-696.

White, Edmund and Dale Brown, The First Men: The Emergence of Man.
     New York: Time-Life Books, 1973.

INDEX

W

BOOKS MAKE GREAT GIFTS

If you would like to order additional copies of this book for family members or friends, send $8.95 plus $1.00 postage and handling to:

Patrick Publications, Dept. 111
P. O. Box 96297
Las Vegas, Nevada 89193-6297

Orders will be shipped within three days of receiving.